STAGE LIGHTING

for

THE AMATEUR PRODUCER

STAGE LIGHTING
for
THE AMATEUR PRODUCER

BY

ANGUS WILSON

WITH A CHAPTER ON LIGHTING FOR PLAYS IN CHURCHES

BY

The Rev. P. Bullock-Flint

FOREWORD BY

E. MARTIN BROWNE

LONDON
SIR ISAAC PITMAN & SONS, LTD.

First published 1960

SIR ISAAC PITMAN & SONS, LTD.
PITMAN HOUSE, PARKER STREET, KINGSWAY, LONDON, W.C.2
THE PITMAN PRESS, BATH
PITMAN HOUSE, BOUVERIE STREET, CARLTON, MELBOURNE
22-25 BECKETT'S BUILDINGS, PRESIDENT STREET, JOHANNESBURG

ASSOCIATED COMPANIES
PITMAN MEDICAL PUBLISHING COMPANY, LTD.
39 PARKER STREET, LONDON, W.C.2

PITMAN PUBLISHING CORPORATION
2 WEST 45TH STREET, NEW YORK

SIR ISAAC PITMAN & SONS (CANADA), LTD.
(INCORPORATING THE COMMERCIAL TEXT BOOK COMPANY)
PITMAN HOUSE, 381-383 CHURCH STREET, TORONTO

MADE IN GREAT BRITAIN AT THE PITMAN PRESS, BATH
Fo—(G.441)

Foreword

AMONG amateur producers there are two points of view about lighting. A considerable number of them understand its possibilities and have taken trouble—often great trouble—to learn something about its nature. From some of these producers come lighting plots as interesting as many of those used in the professional theatre, with the added merit that great difficulties have been overcome to produce the right atmosphere in their productions.

The other class is, I am afraid, larger: and over many years of seeing festivals and other amateur shows I have often sorrowed at the damage which is done to play and acting, let alone setting, by the point of view which these producers take. It is one of despair. Lighting is a mystery which they feel themselves unable to plumb. I am continually surprised at the frequency with which I am told, "the producer sent no lighting plot" for a show.

If some of these producers could be given enough confidence to spur them on towards acquiring an elementary grasp of lighting principles, amateur drama could be immeasurably improved. It is in this hope that I commend Mr. Angus Wilson's little book.

He has tackled the problem boldly and realistically, putting himself in the place of the producer who knows nothing of lighting, and leading him (or her) encouragingly by the hand, step by step. The surrender represented by the despairing cry "I leave it to you, Joe," may now be converted into an explanation which will enable Joe to co-operate in obtaining the best value from whatever lighting plant he has available, according to the requirements of each play.

In the end, everyone will be grateful to Mr. Wilson—producers, actors, designers and, above all, audiences.

E. MARTIN BROWNE

Contents

Illustrations

9

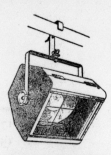

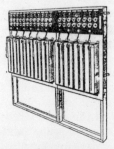

1

Introductory

FOR many producers, especially women, stage lighting is a mystery which there seems little hope of penetrating. It is an affair in which technical terms are muttered by one electrical expert to another, any timid request from the producer being met with shrugs and jargon-laden explanations of why it can't be done. She (sometimes he) retires baffled, and decides to "leave it to Joe."

Now the Joes of the amateur stage are mostly fine technicians, able to do wonders with inadequate equipment, but they are seldom artists in light. When the curtain goes up the play is visible to the audience, but all the producer's efforts to create the visual feeling and mood that the play demands are ruined by a flat blaze that shows up everything in one dimension, or by harsh murkiness caused by the wrong use of coloured gelatines. A school caretaker many years ago switched on everything and said to me: "Marvellous, isn't it? Not a shadow anywhere!" This ideal, just right for a hospital's operating theatre, is less widespread than it was, but it is far from extinct. Leaving it to Joe is generally fatal to theatrical art.

The lighting of a play should be thought out and visualized by no one but the producer, along with scenery, costume, props and make-up, but, of all these, it is by far the most difficult to imagine. When you go to anyone else's play, the other things are visible (and tangible if you go back stage) but you see only the subtle results of good lighting—you have no means of knowing how it is done. In the early stages of your own production, you can discuss the designs, submitted by your artist or wardrobe mistress, but when Joe drifts up to you and says: "What do you want in the way of lighting, Miss?"

how can you exchange ideas when *he* cannot bring you a drawing and *you* cannot make up a light-plot? How can you translate your vision into instructions that Joe will understand and be able to carry out? Can you do this without a lot of technical knowledge?

It is the purpose of this book to help you to solve these problems, to show you that lighting is not an electrical mystery and to encourage you to take it in your stride along with the other aspects of production. I hope to hear you say, two or three productions from now: "I know scarcely anything about electricity—a bus-bar sounds to me like a place where buses line up to get petrol—*but I know what lighting I want and how to get it.*"

2

Aims

I shall begin with the basic requirements of good stage lighting. They are, in order of importance—

(*a*) Visibility of all that is meant to be seen, especially the actors.

(*b*) Subtle help in the creation of the mood and emotional impact of the play.

(*c*) Contrast and emphasis which make the whole scene so much more interesting to look at, as for instance, when persons, objects or areas stand out against darker backgrounds. When you emphasize by light people or things that are concerned in the high moments of drama, you are making the audience concentrate.

(*d*) Colour, which can help the work of your scene-painter and costumier to give some naturalism to such things as sunset and moonlight, and assist aims (*b*) and (*c*).

(*e*) Good technical management, such as dimming, switching on and off table-lamps to cue and so on. (Joe seldom lets you down in things like these.)

(*f*) Unobtrusiveness. The lighting must serve the production and not be an object of special notice and admiration. I place this last because no one needs the warning until after his second or third successfully-lit show; then he often becomes conceited and longs to hear, "Wasn't the lighting wonderful?" If that is his hope, he has failed as a producer and as a lighting artist.

All these points, incidentally, are a valuable part of your own playgoing equipment. Look for them the next time you see a play.

3

How to Learn

GOING to good productions does not help a beginner very much, but bad ones, where you can gleefully say: "Wasn't the lighting awful? I'm sure I can do better than that," are much more instructive, in a negative way. At least they show you what to avoid.

If you see a well-lit amateur show, you can sometimes go round afterwards and ask the producer and the electrician how it was done—we are always glad to show off—but that is not much good if the switchboard is dead and everyone is wanting to go home: make arrangements beforehand with the producer.

Several stage-lighting firms have demonstration theatres fitted up with everything they produce, and the men in charge are always willing to put on a display for you, and advise you what to get for your stage, even if all you can afford at the moment is one small flood.

Drama organizations frequently arrange lecture-demonstrations on lighting. These can be admirable when the stage is well equipped, but it often happens that the only one available has a lighting set that is almost useless for this purpose, and the unfortunate lecturer can do little to avoid disappointing you. I have had to demonstrate far oftener with poor equipment than with good, so you should not rely on such events for your education.

Books such as those listed on page 80 will tell you much, but by far the best way to learn is to reserve an evening or two on some stage which has spots, floods, sky-cloth lights and good dimming equipment, and persuade Joe to show you how everything works and to carry out any experiments you may fancy. As this will involve changing gelatines and angles

of throw, with much step-ladder work, take a few helpers
with you so that Joe can stay at his switchboard. If you can
have a rudimentary set with flats and furniture erected so
much the better; it can be cleared away when you want to
get on to lighting of exteriors and to sky effects.

Such an evening is enormously exhilarating, and from then
on you will be much better able to visualize the lighting of
your next play and plan it so that final rehearsals will go
smoothly and happily.

4

Technical

IT is hardly possible to arrange the lighting of a play without some knowledge of what the different kinds of apparatus can and cannot do. Fortunately it doesn't matter twopence if you can't tell a volt from a lampholder—that is Joe's business—but if you want a certain effect it is much better to be able to say, for example, "I think a pageant lantern will do it. Let's start with that anyhow." Technicians hate vagueness and messing about, but if you have a definite preliminary idea, they are always happy to help you to change it if it doesn't work.

All stage lights fall into two broad categories, concentrated and diffused.

CONCENTRATED LIGHTING

These units throw a beam of light which can be directed on any object or area and which illuminates nothing else.

The commonest and most valuable are spotlights. (The correct name for these is focus lights because the lamp shines through a lens which can to some extent be focused, but the former term is more frequently used, abbreviated to "spots.") The type of spot which was universal on amateur stages till a few years ago is shown in Fig. 1 (a). The principal thing a producer needs to know about it is that its beam can be made to spread at a wide angle over the stage or to give a disc of more intense light not much larger than the lens itself. If it exactly covers a small table and you want to include all the people sitting round, say: "Can I have a wider spread, please?" Remember, however, that the wider the spread the weaker the light.

is often useful to have a small spot which can be concealed
ne footlights or behind a waste-paper basket or arm-chair,
heightening the contrast on some object not more than
ut fifteen feet away. The Float Spotlight, which is about
n. × 8 in. × 5½ in. does this job very neatly.

ig. 1 (b) shows the Mirror Spot, which differs from the
er kind in that (a) it gives a more intense light from the
ne strength of lamp and is therefore more economical; (b)
beam can be left in its original roundness or shaped by
sks into a square or rectangle; (c) it can have an iris
phragm which, as in a camera, cuts down the beam and
n do the work of a dimmer; (a) and (b) make it particularly
luable for fitting up as Front of House lighting (F.O.H.)
t in the auditorium, since the longer throw may not need a
ronger lamp, and the beam can be shaped to fit the pro-
enium opening with no irritating spill at top and sides.
.O.H. serves to light the actor who is down stage under the
ain lights, or out beyond the proscenium on the fore stage
c apron.)

Two other kinds of concentrated lighting units give a beam
vhich lacks the sharp cut-off of the lens lanterns, but as their
pill is very small they can be justifiably included.

One is the Soft Focus (Fresnel) Spot, shown in Fig. 1 (c).
This has a flat prismatic lens-plate instead of the plano-
convex type of the normal spot, and it is claimed that it passes
much more light. It gives a brilliant circle of light which
shades off rapidly all round instead of leaving the hard edge
of the normal spot lens, and it is particularly good when used
as F.O.H. close up to the proscenium. From farther off, its
spill is liable to show all round the edges. On stage it can be
used very effectively in the ordinary way.

The other is the Pageant Lantern (Fig. 1 (d)), which has no
lens but is deep enough to keep most of the light in a brilliant
shaft. This cannot be varied greatly in spread, but it is
excellent for simulating sun or moon, and can be used either
from up behind the proscenium, or on a stand through a
window or between wings.

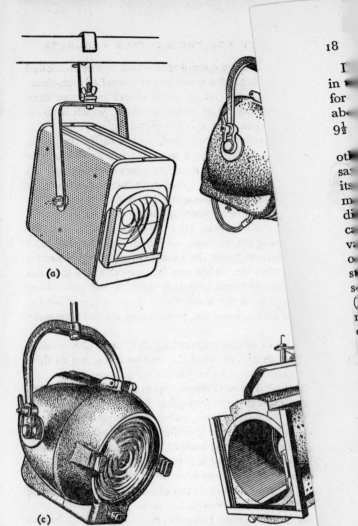

FIG. 1. SPOTLIGHTS

(a) Standard Type Spot (250/500-watt).
(b) 250/500-watt Baby Mirror Spot for F.O.H. positions.
(c) 250/500-watt Fresnel Spot giving soft-edged beam.
(d) Pageant.

(*Courtesy of Strand Electric and Engineering Co. Ltd.*)

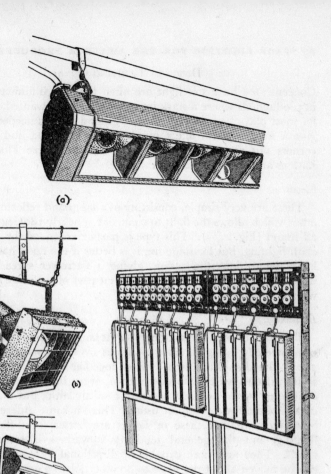

FIG. 2. DIFFUSED LIGHTING AND SWITCHBOARD

(a) Batten.
(b) Wide angle flood.
(c) 60/200-watt Junior Flood with hood for restricting spread of light when required.
(d) 20 circuit/10 dimmers Junior Board with plugging system.

(*Courtesy of Strand Electric and Engineering Co. Ltd.*)

DIFFUSED LIGHTING

Concentrated beams of light are often the only illumination in productions where a stark impressionist look is wanted, but for most plays a certain amount of general light is needed to give a more natural effect by showing the setting and the corners not reached by the spots. This is where Floods, Battens and Footlights are invaluable.

Floods

These are very simple, consisting of a lamp and reflector in a box which allows the light to come out at nearly 180 degrees all round (Fig. 2 (b)). This type is particularly good for sky-cloth lighting, but for stage use it is better if the flood has its lamp deeper into the casing, giving a narrower spread of light and allowing some choice of what part of the stage you wish to emphasize (Fig. 2 (c)).

Battens

These are rows of 100-watt or 75-watt lamps, each in its own compartment, hung in fixed positions over the stage (Fig. 2 (a)). The lamps are usually wired together in three groups, so that if one switch is pressed down, every third lamp will come on. It can be every second or fourth lamp, but three-circuit battens are the most usual. There is some difference of opinion whether these or floods are better for diffused lighting, but the general tendency nowadays is towards floods. They are more capable of directional lighting, and can be moved about the stage to do other jobs. Their colour mediums can be changed more easily and quickly; in short, floods are more flexible.

The three-colour system in battens is dealt with on page 36.

Footlights

These, often called "floats," are the simplest to rig up of all stage lights, but among the most difficult to use properly. Their function is to give some light to the under surfaces of the actors' faces when these are in deep shadow from the overhead lights. They should provide a more natural balance, that is all. It is a lamentably common fault of amateur lighting to have the floats so strong that they light the actors' legs, the lower sides of the furniture, and the upper works of the stage, while casting tall shadows on the setting or the sky-cloth. Their total length should be no more than two-thirds of the proscenium opening, to avoid ugly shadows on the sides of the setting.

Sky-cloth Lighting

Strictly speaking, a sky-cloth is flat and a cyclorama, or "cyc," is curved, either all round or only at the ends, but the term cyc is often used for all sky-cloths, flat or curved. A backcloth usually bears a painted scene, and as this is rather difficult for most societies to achieve, I shall deal only with a plain cloth meant to represent the sky when lit. This should be carefully stretched so as to be free of wrinkles[1] and dis-tempered white or very pale blue.

The sky-cloth can be lit by either battens or floods. I have a slight preference for a long batten, as it gives a very even distribution of light and of colour. Floods must be of the wide-angle variety to avoid patchiness, but there is, otherwise, very little difference.

Good top lighting will reach to the bottom of the cloth if it is the proper distance away from it, but even if it fades off some-what no harm is done, because our skies are always bluer at the zenith than at the horizon. But if you want sunrises and sunsets you should have some wide-angle floods ready to throw up a pink-amber glow from behind a groundrow.

Before you start to install any sky-cloth lighting, make sure that your electrician and your Treasurer understand that it needs about as much wattage as all the diffused lighting (battens, floods, footlights) that is likely to fall on it from the other lighting positions. It does not matter much if actors'

[1] For methods of hanging, see my *Scenic Equipment for the Small Stage*, p. 41 (Allen and Unwin).

shadows fall on flats or curtains, but it is fatal to allow them on the "sky"; the sky-cloth lighting must be strong enough to kill them.

Strip Lights

Every stage should have a few odd lengths of wood fitted with lampholders for lighting backings to door and windows and for various odd jobs; coloured lamps are quite adequate for these.

Gelatines

It is Joe's business to obtain and fit them, and their colour is dealt with in a later section, but you should insist on his having a good supply of Frosted Gelatine, known as Frosts, to soften the hard edge of a spotlight beam. A small irregular hole in the centre will allow the full power of the lamp in the centre of the circle, while maintaining diffusion at the outside edge.

SWITCHBOARDS, WIRING, DIMMERS

As these are highly technical, they also are in Joe's domain. If, however, you are called in to help plan a set of equipment, ask for flexibility in the dimming arrangements. This means that any dimmer can be plugged into any circuit and a few dimmers can therefore do a great deal of work. You will be told that it is no good expecting a 1,000-watt dimmer to check a 150-watt lamp, it just won't make any difference, and it is highly dangerous to try dimming 1,000 watts on a 150-watt dimmer, so that complete interchangeability is seldom possible. But compromises can be made, and the chief point is to avoid the sort of board on which each dimmer is wired permanently to a circuit and cannot be used for any other. The technical books describe a wide variety of flexible boards, and your electrician should study them. A useful type of board is shown in Fig. 2 (d).

Wiring also is not your affair, but ask for some "dips" on the stage. These are sockets, wired to the board, sunk just under the floorboards at various points outside the acting area.

They are extremely useful for plugging in floods, strip lights and anything that has no permanent position.

Building up

A wonderful day may dawn when you are in a position to advise on how a fair sum of money should be spent on lighting equipment. You cannot go into detail with the technicians, but you can say firmly in what order of priority the various items of equipment should be considered. The greater part of the money should be allocated to—

Spots (Stage and F.O.H.)
Switchboard
Dimmers
Wiring
Floods
Sky-cloth lights

in that order. Footlights can easily be left out till finances build up again, or can be omitted altogether, and battens can take the place of floods if preferred.

But there never may be such a glorious day. How then will you start, when you have only a few pounds?

Here is a scheme of progression for a company with a small stage, a 15-amp supply (as for heating at home) and nothing else—

1. Two 500-watt spots (in the "primary positions" described on page 30) wired straight to the supply and adjusted to give the widest possible beam.

2. A simple flexible switchboard with, say, six circuits and two dimmers, capable of being added to.

3. Two floods of 250 or 200 watts.

4. Two 500-watt mirror spots as F.O.H.

5. More circuits and dimmers on the switchboard. By this time, 15 amps will not be enough, so you must start negotiations with your electricity authority. A new meter will certainly be needed, and, if you mean to end up with a really complete lighting set, you had better ask for a supply of between 100 and 150 amps.

6. One or two spots for stage.

7. Upper sky-cloth batten, or row of four to six floods.

8. Two or four dips.

9. Some more floods for stage.

10. Spots *ad lib.* for stage and F.O.H.

11. About now you may have to remodel the old bits-and-pieces board with a generous supply of extra circuits beyond the maximum you think you will need. A master dimmer and submasters should be added if possible.

12. Lower sky-cloth batten; acting-area lantern; pageant lantern, etc.

Strip lights can be added at any time. You will, of course, adapt this scheme to suit your circumstances, but the main point is that concentrated light should come first, with diffused light taking a secondary place. Keep in mind that you can hire equipment at reasonable rates from the firms that advertise in amateur dramatic magazines (*see also* list at end); thus you need not be prevented from doing an occasional play that needs more apparatus than you can afford to buy at that moment. Also, ingenious mechanics with some spare time can make a surprising amount of equipment, as explained in my book *Home-made Lighting Apparatus for the Amateur Stage*.

NOTE ON WATTS AND AMPS

I have assumed hitherto that you will not be attempting to bandy technicalities with those who know more than you, but it happens now and then that an electrician, especially if he is new to you, may say that his fuses will not stand any more lamps, whereas you are pretty sure they will. If you can find out what the supply to the fuse or to the whole switchboard is in terms of amps (amperes, the rate of flow of current), and the voltage (unit of pressure of supply), you can find out how many watts (unit of power or strength of lamp) the fuse or the board will take.

The formula is Watts = Volts × Amps, but here is a table that will provide a quick reference. The amps column shows the commonest rating of fuses.

Volts	Amps	Watts
200–220	5	1,000–1,100
	13	2,600–2,860
	15	3,000–3,300
230–250	5	1,150–1,250
	13	2,990–3,250
	15	3,450–3,750

Direct Current (D.C.) is mostly at 200–220 volts;
Alternating Current (A.C.) at 230–250 volts.

5

Positions of Lights

WHEN you stage your play in a hired hall you must usually take the lighting equipment as you find it. Some small alterations may be possible, but the location of the various units can seldom be altered.

On your own stage, however, you can place them where you please, and correct positioning is an important part of lighting technique.

FACE-LEVEL LIGHTING

If you shine a light down on a face from almost vertical, the eye-sockets are in deep shadow, the cheek-bones stand out, there are strong shadows below the nose and lower lip. Occasionally, this is the skeletal effect you want, but mostly it is unfair to the face and the actor behind it.

From below, the shadows and highlights are reversed, and the result is even more sinister—just the thing for a horror play about men from Mars. Lit from directly in front, the face is an expressionless blank, without character, rather like a criminal's identity photograph.

But place your light so that its beam is somewhere between 30 degrees and 45 degrees to the horizontal and the face becomes that of a human being, with shadows of the right depth and in the right places. Put two lights at the same height as before but away to the sides, with gelatines slightly different in tint, and the effect is even better; the shadows are now subtly contrasted in two shades, each differing from the highlights where the colours are mixed.

If stage lighting were only a matter of showing one static face, as in a photograph, this section would be superfluous, but the faces move about from right to left, and from the front of the fore-stage to just below the backcloth. How then can we look after the modelling?

The answer is that we can do it only in a rough-and-ready manner, by ensuring that no light on stage or F.O.H. is mounted at face level, and that the approximate angle already mentioned is observed as far as possible.

Thus, face-level lights are liable to be found mostly as F.O.H. when the ceiling of the hall is low or when the lights

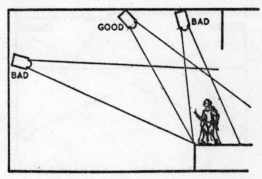

FIG. 3. ANGLE OF FRONT OF HOUSE LIGHTS

Good and bad angles for three spots hung along the central line of the auditorium ceiling.

are too far from the stage, for instance, at the top of the back wall of the auditorium.

In two amateur theatres I know well I have seen F.O.H. blazing away at only about 22 degrees, giving that criminal look to any actor unlucky enough to be down-stage of the main lighting. If your hall ceiling is low, place any centre F.O.H. at the distance from the stage which will give you the best angle (see Fig. 3). If the ceiling is high and cannot easily be reached by ladders, avoid the temptation to put in strong spots on the back wall, for the angle is sure to be wrong unless the hall is very short, but put them on the side walls as high as possible and as near the proscenium as you can (see Fig. 4).

Lack of height matters much less if the light is coming from the side; shadows, especially of the nose, may seem a little unnatural, but they are better than none at all.

The wrong use of footlights has already been dealt with on page 21, and to that should be added the use of floods standing on the stage in the wings to light the actors. They not only give face-level effects but show up actors at the sides of the stage more strongly than those in the centre. Further, a

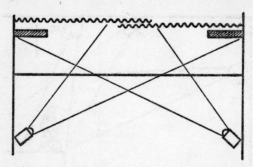

FIG. 4. FRONT OF HOUSE LIGHTS ON SIDE WALLS

These F.O.H. Spots, hung as high as possible, cover most of the fore-stage.

broad-shouldered man standing supposedly unnoticed at the side may be completely blocking off a light meant for someone else. So, if you have to use floods from this position, hoist them to at least 7 ft. These strictures do not of course apply when floods are used to shine through windows, etc., and suggest sunshine and moonshine. These must be at whatever height the source of light is supposed to be; for example, low for sunrise or sunset, high for noon.

No. 1 Batten

These low-trajectory lights which threaten to flatten our stage picture are mostly F.O.H. spots, footlights and stage-level floods. What of the rest? In Fig. 5 a side view of the standard arrangement of lights over the stage is shown, the

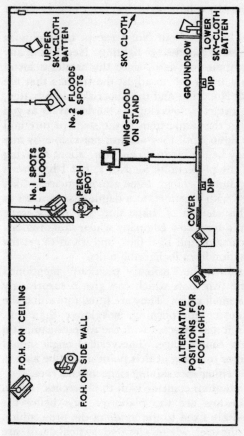

FIG. 5. SECTIONAL VIEW OF LIGHTING SET

Rough sketch, not to scale and omitting curtains and borders, of the positions of units lighting a stage which is over 12 ft deep and has a fore-stage. When there is no fore-stage the footlights will be fitted in the left-hand alternative position; when fore-stage is in use they will be removed or sunk, and the cover put over.

most important being the row just behind the pelmet (or the upper part of the proscenium). This was called for many years No. 1 Batten, but since battens are steadily being replaced by mixed spots and floods, a new name has been found—No. 1 Bar.

Not much need be said about No. 1 except to emphasize a point which applies to all on-stage lighting. Never have any units hung higher than you need, since this wastes a lot of light-power. It is a tricky job to adjust the borders that are required to conceal No. 2 bar and the upper sky-cloth batten, but you can make a start by lowering the borders as far as you can without spoiling the proportions of the stage picture and then lowering the lights until they are just not visible by any spectator. You may be unable to do anything about lowering the upper part of the proscenium for No. 1, but I have seen many lofty proscenium openings, some almost square, which could well be fitted with a pelmet, to a depth of sometimes as much as 6 ft. This change of shape may not please some spectators, but it is a boon to a company which cannot afford enormously long curtains and 18-ft flats, and wants to get the maximum illumination from its lighting units.

In Fig. 6 are shown the "primary positions" mentioned on page 23 for the two spots which can give a surprisingly effective light on a small stage. They are fitted up behind the corners of the proscenium opening, not lower than 7 ft, preferably 8 ft or 9 ft and directed with the widest beam, at a point a little below centre stage. The vertical angle should be such that an actor standing at that point should be able to see the lamp inside either spot shining right into his eyes.

These primary positions coincide with the "perches" which in professional theatres are the platforms, one being the electrician's, which are fixed to the inside of the proscenium. In the amateur theatre, where elevated switchboards are regrettably few, the term applies to any spot which is fixed up behind the proscenium corners.

The lanterns in No. 1 bar should hang from a tube, which in turn hangs from cables—ropes are dangerous—passing over pulleys in the stage ceiling. Thus, the whole thing can be lowered to man level for adjustment, change of gelatine, cleaning and so on. If you cannot have pulleys, do not despair;

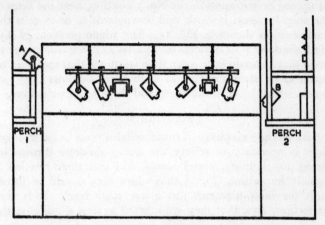

FIG. 6. NO. 1 BAR FROM UP-STAGE

View of stage, looking from back wall towards proscenium. No. 1 bar is made up of any number of spots and floods, all directable. *A* and *B* are the "primary positions" mentioned on page 23 and are shown in two different situations on the perches.

it is nearly always possible to fix spots and floods to the inside of the upper proscenium, provided it is within ladder reach.

No. 2 Bar

In Fig. 5, a No. 2 is shown. On a shallow stage, say, only 12 ft from sky-cloth to front curtain, No. 1 will adequately light actors standing up stage, but where the distance is greater, these actors will tend to be only half lit, in irritating contrast with those nearer centre. You must decide for yourself whether your stage needs a No. 2. It is usually composed of the same units as No. 1, with fewer spots.

Your decision will depend to some extent on whether you are using a backcloth as open sky in outdoor scenes, because the floods from No. 2 bar will inevitably throw actors' shadows on it. Powerful sky-cloth lighting will kill them, but you may not be able to achieve such strength, and you would do better to fit up one or two spots in the No. 2 position, near the sides of the stage, trained inwards and downwards so as to miss the backcloth, as shown in Fig. 13. The whole problem of sky-cloth shadows is so intricate and varies so much from stage to stage that I can do little more than warn you that spots can be much more easily directed so as to avoid shadows than can floods, which by their nature spread their light everywhere.

FOOTLIGHTS

I have already emphasized that footlights must be no stronger than is necessary to relieve the heavy shadows thrown by strong top lighting, and I would add that their position is equally important. Fig. 5 shows how they should be fitted, with the lamp-filaments just above stage level. It is very important, also, that they are masked against shining on the upper part of the proscenium.

When your actors are to move from the main acting area to a fore-stage, they cannot step over the footlights. These must, therefore, be sunk, with a lid over the trough which is lifted when the fore-stage is not being used. Incidentally, a fore stage is useless without good F.O.H. lighting.

SKY-CLOTH BATTENS

The positions of these should be clear from Fig. 5, but make sure that the angle of throw and the distance from the cloth are such as to give an even flood all over. A good deal of experiment and adjustment is required, and it should be noted that the lower batten is as *high* as possible behind the ground-row.

ARENA PRODUCTION

This type of work (known also as Open Stage or Playing in the Round) is usually done in the middle of the auditorium with the audience on at least three sides. There is no argument about what sort of units to use—they must be spots, as anything else will shine into the spectators' eyes. The spots will be hung from the hall ceiling, or from any balconies there may be, and directed down on the acting area. The angles and beam-spreads must be very carefully adjusted so as to light the actors and no one else.

The obvious conclusion is that you should not attempt arena staging unless you can fulfil the above conditions. Of course, if you don't mind how your production is lit, then do it in the normal hall lighting, but, having seen arena work under both kinds of lighting, I have no hesitation in saying that I'd rather see a play normally staged than have all illusion destroyed by finding myself in the same illumination as the players.

6

Colour

COLOUR, in spite of a good deal of pretentious writing on the subject, is much less important in lighting most plays than intensity and direction. These give contrast and life to what the audience sees, whereas the addition of colour does little more than soften the harshness and dullness of white light and make the whole effect more pleasant to look at. Now and then, of course, you see a chance, perhaps in a short scene of a non-realistic play, to heighten the emotional impact by using strong colours carefully chosen to symbolize Death or Jealousy or Horror, and in ballet this is done continually, but for the greater part of the drama that appears in both amateur and professional theatres, the deep red and the crossed beams of purple and vivid green would be ludicrously out of place.

Furthermore, the strong colours cut off an enormous amount of light, and you must buy many more lamps and use much more current if you are to make your actors visible. Get samples of gelatines from one of the stage-lighting firms, and you can test this for yourself at home.

Colours such as deep green and orange have an effect on make-up similar to that of sodium or mercury-vapour street lighting; and what actress wants to look like a cadaver? A brilliant green costume in a deep mauve light looks a dirty grey, to the despair and rage of the wardrobe-mistress. Also, it is absurd in a naturalistic play to see the characters stepping from one pool of vivid pink down left to another of equally vivid magenta down centre.

To go to the other extreme, you can do without colour altogether if your lights are very weak, only just strong enough to show your actors and their surroundings. The light from ordinary electric lamps has a good deal of red in it, and will give a pleasant effect if its strength is low. It is also possible to buy household lamps which are tinted slightly pink, and these would be quite adequate for a straightforward scene on a stage where, for example, a 5-amp supply allows you to use only ten or eleven lamps of 100 watts each. There are still a few unfortunate village and church hall stages which have no more than this.

CHOICE OF GELATINE COLOUR

When you study the list of about fifty colours that accompanies the gelatine samples mentioned on page 34, you will be rather bewildered by its extent and variety. In fact, you will need only about a dozen of them, with a few extra for special purposes. Here are those you are most likely to require, with the effects they give—

Warm		*Neutral*		*Cold*	
Light Rose	7	Pale Yellow	50	Steel Blue	17
Pale Salmon	53	Straw	3	Pale Lavender	36
Middle Rose	10	Pale Gold	52	Blue Grey	44
Gold Tint	51			Pale Green	38

Others for special duties are—

Dark Pink	11 ⎫ fire	Dark Blue	19	Night sky
Deep Amber	33 ⎭	Light Blue	40	and day sky.
Deep Orange	5a (with 11), sunset			

Note the absence from the general list of amber, a colour still used far too much by amateurs. It appears to simulate sunshine or warm interior light, but it makes faces look harsh, lined and old, and kills any colour in costume and set except yellow and some of the reds. Strong green has a similar effect, and though I have listed Pale Green among the cold colours, it should be used only after careful experiment and always in combination with other colours. Indeed, no colour should ever be used alone, for, no matter how pleasant it is, it will seem drab and uninteresting if there is no contrast. Flood your stage with light rose if you wish, but have steel and lavender in your spots to liven up faces. What I wrote on page 26 about the effects of differently coloured shadows on the face applies very strongly here, and you can play about endlessly with such mixtures, using light rose and gold in your floods, with straw and pale green in your spots, or the other way round. I shall have more to say about colour in the Chapter "Lighting Your Play," but I urge you not to make a fetish of it. You can be so subtle and symbolic that not one member of your audience has any notion of what you're getting at. If you wish to go deeply into theory, you will find it in most advanced handbooks on Stage Lighting, but I am convinced that time spent on such research is seldom justified by the results the spectator sees and appreciates, and is better used on more important aspects of production.

THREE-COLOUR BATTENS

You will find many stages equipped with what is known as the three-colour system. Every batten has three circuits, each fitted with one of the three primary colours, red, green and deep blue, and each circuit on a dimmer. When all are at full power, white (or nearly white) light floods the stage. By altering the intensity of the primaries, you can get any colour you like. This was once considered to be a valuable system, but experience has shown that it is extremely wasteful. The deep colours of the gelatines cut off a fantastic proportion of the possible illumination, and an enormous number of lamps must be used to get a result that is anything more than murky. If you find this state of affairs, get the electrician to substitute pale gelatines in whatever colours you have chosen for your general lighting, and you can use each circuit as if it were a single flood. Suppose you decide on light blue, straw and rose, you can have them checked respectively to one quarter, one-half, and just below full. This, after experiment and further

adjustment will give a soft evening light with plenty of brightness. For daylight, bring up the blue and straw to full and
check the rose a little; for moonlight, light blue only, with
perhaps one compartment carrying steel to add whiteness.
Thus, by planning ahead, you can get far better results than
the pure three-colour system will give you.

7

Miscellaneous Effects

STAGE lighting need not be all work and worry. You can have plenty of fun adapting your apparatus to create illusions which are enjoyed by the audience and are yet a legitimate part of the play's artistic impact. Here are some of the commonest examples.

SKY

Some authorities say that a pale blue cloth needs only white light, but I have found that such a cloth tends to look washed-out and grey. This is excellent when the stage weather is supposed to be rainy and dull, but for normal sky, it is better to use blue in the battens or floods. Middle Blue 18 should be tried first, changing to the darker Medium Blue 32 or lighter Steel Blue 17 if necessary.

If you have night sky and day sky in the same play, the colouring of the top batten may cause some difficulty, since the deep blue of a night sky can be obtained only by using Dark Blue 19 or Primary Blue 20 and these require a dispropor-tionate amount of your available wattage. I can only suggest that you experiment with the colours mentioned above and the Blues 17, 18 and 32 that give the effect of day sky to find the balance that best suits your circumstances. Of course, if the play needs only one sort of sky, there is no problem.

SUNRISE AND SUNSET

The latter (more commonly seen on stages than sunrise) should start with a gentle blush of Dark Pink 11 which, as it grows stronger, is joined by an equal wattage of Deep Orange 5a, both being brought up to the strength required. Then the orange is faded out, leaving the pink to fade out in its turn. The relative strength of the colours and the changes in intensity required are, of course, to be discovered by trial and error, but the main point is that nearly all sunsets have a lot of yellow in them and not much pure red.

Any floods can be used, behind a groundrow (*see* Fig. 5) for this purpose, or a strip of open coloured bulbs, since there is no need to spread your sunset all along the cloth. Since the stage sun cannot be shown coming down the middle of the sky-cloth, it is more realistic to have it setting at one end of the groundrow, as if it had been shining from off stage all after-noon.

As I have seldom seen a genuine sunrise from start to finish, I can only assume that the process on stage is the same as for sunset. I must get up early one morning and look.

Night and Moonlight

Unfortunately for dramatic purposes, real night is just black-ness, so we must bow to necessity and make our actors visible. Use blue, not green, and err on the side of too much light rather than too little. Nothing is more irritating for an audience than having to strain their eyes during a long scene in the effort to see which character is speaking, and they cannot be blamed if they stop listening. You can always add moon-light unless the author says you must not, and this again is not green, or even blue-green. It is in nature pure white, which is best represented by Steel 17 from a spot or pageant-lantern high up. A rising moon can be shown by a lamp in a circular tin covered by frosted gelatine, held against the back of the sky-cloth and moved slowly up, but such devices have a horrible fascination for any playgoer (who is always hoping it will jerk or begin to go down again), and are, like children and animals, unfair to actors. You can start your moonrise with a weak flood at face level off-stage, fading it as your high lamp is brought up on the dimmer—this is not fully realistic, but is perfectly acceptable.

FIRE

Once again, fire is often wrongly represented as a deep ruby red. It should be mixed pale pink and light amber when the flames are supposed to be leaping (there are many simple devices to give the flickering effect), dying down to medium or deep pink when only embers are left. Off-stage fires follow the same routine, and are best done by using one or two floods on stands.

MISTS AND GHOSTS

Though this book does not deal with "stage effects," there are a few that involve lighting. One of the most important uses theatrical gauze, obtainable from dealers in stage equipment, which has the property of being opaque when lit from in front and transparent when lit from behind. A ghost can thus stand invisible behind a piece of gauze painted to look like a door or an arras, and be revealed when the main lighting is dimmed and his own lights brought up.

A backcloth or groundrow can be made to disappear into "mist" if a large sheet of gauze is hung in front, and the back lighting brought down slowly. For fuller details see *Stage Lighting* by Geoffrey Ost and several other textbooks.

LIGHTNING

Carbon arcs were often used to give the required flickering flash, but they need such careful handling that it is better to get one or two photographer's photo-flood lamps, fit them into an open-fronted box, and switch them on and off rapidly and irregularly. If your electrician can rig up a push button for their control, so much the better, as some types of switch are apt to be noisy.

For an interior setting, the box should be placed off-stage, high up, so that the light can shine on sky-cloth, groundrow, etc., with some of it coming in through the windows and open doors. For an exterior, have the box rigged somewhere on No. 1 bar.

Conventions

Just as the playgoer accepts the proscenium opening as an imaginary fourth wall to a box-set, so he accepts certain unrealistic features of lighting. Few places in real life are lit powerfully from above in one direction only, but as there is no substitute for the No. 1 and F.O.H. positions in lighting, he must agree to forget that also.

But do not trade too much on your spectator's complaisance. Do not expect him to ignore a sunset through the window stage left quickly followed by a moonrise through the same window, or a fire half-way up-stage left with the glow coming from behind the proscenium.

Only careless producers would offer such crudities, but many neglect to take advantage of some devices which help illusion. When, for instance, you have carefully arranged for sunshine from a flood or pageant to pour in at a window in the left wall of the set, see that the main lighting which is directed across the stage from left is lighter in tone, or stronger than that coming in the opposite direction. The result will be that an actor anywhere on the stage will have more and paler light on his face when he is looking towards the window than when he is looking away. Unfortunately, this dodge is pointless if the window is in the back wall.

Similarly, firelight coming out of the fireplace from a spot or flood is often reinforced by a shaft of warm-tinted light coming from a spot trained on the area in front of the fireplace (*see* Fig. 12) and a table-lamp should also have a pool of light round it. The last two examples are somewhat less naturalistic in effect than the sunshine trick, but they are accepted as conventions and are a valuable help to the creation of contrast and emphasis.

8

Lighting Your Play

I SHOULD dearly love to draw up some clever diagrammatic device whereby you could follow lines and columns and have a complete light scheme for any play at the turn of a handle, as it were. Since this is obviously impossible, I shall divide all drama into rough and arbitrary categories and advise you on the basic principles of lighting plays which can be fitted into them. I need not stress that this will be only very general guidance, or that many plays come into more than one of my divisions.

REALIST INTERIORS

For probably three-quarters of the total time of curtain-up in the amateur theatre, audiences are looking at one of these; this is a pity, for by the time you have come to the end of this chapter you will agree that the kitchen, or drawing-room, or library, or lounge-hall is much the least interesting and rewarding to the lighting artist, just as it is to the scenic artist. But the fact is inescapable, so we turn our attention to the impression the actor is trying to make on his spectators and help him all we can.

Farces and Light Comedies

Most of these can be dismissed in a few words—brightness, cheerfulness, and maximum visibility. Leave it to Joe, specifying only that his footlights should be at a little less than their usual fierce blaze, just as a slight concession to naturalism. Otherwise, on with the wattage!

Serious Plays

This class ranges from thoughtful comedy through problem plays to high tragedy, and the first essential is to put stronger lights on the actor than on his surroundings. An extreme instance of this would be a monologue said by a character lit by one shaft from a spotlight, the furniture and walls being only faintly discernible.

Normally, you decide what are the areas or pieces of furniture in or on which the main dramatic action is to take place, and make sure that each is covered by a spotlight. If you have enough spots you should direct two of them from different angles on to each of the "highlights," thus giving full and interesting lighting to every face whichever way it may turn (*see* Figs. 7, 8 and 9). Do not forget doors and windows at which people are to make startling entries—your audience won't jump if the actor is only just visible.

When you are happy about this, start to fill in the gaps. If you light an ordinary stage with only four or five spots, you will produce a very patchy picture, with characters moving from bright light into obscurity, so bring up your floods until the setting and unused corners can be comfortably seen. But if the actor is no longer standing out against his background, bring them down again. Keep them off the upper quarter of the setting so that the flats or curtains seem to go up into darkness, and be particularly careful with your footlights lest they undo the good work. Remember what I previously urged about the source of light if it is from a window, fire or lamp (*see* pages 41 and 46) directing and colouring your floods and spots accordingly. Do not be niggardly with wall lights, standard-lamps and chandeliers, but use only low-powered bulbs in them and never allow these to shine directly into the audience's eyes.

Realist interiors are usually in either daylight, evening or artificial light. These can be reproduced quite adequately by the cold, neutral and warm colours listed on page 35, and the next thing is to ensure that the gelatines in the floods which light the scenery do not kill its colours; for example, pink flats will suffer badly under a yellow-green light. Tell your designer what colours you intend to use in your floods and he will paint his set to suit. (He ought to have a sample batch of gelatines so that he can shine a torch through them on to his sketches.)

When you have to move from afternoon to dusk and then to artificial light during the same act it is easy to overlook the fact that gelatines cannot be changed while the curtain is up except in the rare spot or flood which is within your electrician's reach and then only when it has been dimmed out. You will be obliged reluctantly to keep some floods and spots, fitted with warm gelatines, unlit until someone says: "Put on the lights, dear, and draw the curtains." This will be specially annoying if your equipment will only just do the afternoon adequately, but there are two possible ways out. Either set aside your evening lights as already described and increase the power of your few remaining afternoon lights by using the palest possible gelatines or none at all. Or, have them all on for afternoon, then bring down the brightest for dusk and half-way up again for evening. Lamps when dimmed give a somewhat redder light than they do when full up, which helps the "cosy" effect.

A play with a stark and tragic theme does not necessarily need cold gloomy lighting. I have heard of a production of Ibsen's *Ghosts* by Esmé Church in which the settings, costumes and lighting were all as gay and colourful as fidelity to nineteenth-century Norway would allow, the producer arguing that Mrs. Alving was happy for the first time for many years, had her son with her again and was sure of the future. Thus, when the cold hand of the past came to grip her, the contrast of her increasing wretchedness with the cheerfulness of her surroundings was made all the more poignant and dramatic. It is an idea which would not apply to every similar play, but is well worth keeping in mind.

I am sometimes asked: "How much should one vary intensity and colour to fit the mood of the moment? Should one, for instance, isolate Mrs. Alving and her son during their duologues by bringing down everything except two spots, put a rosy pink on them when they are happy and steel or lavender when they are miserable?"

There is no simple answer to this question. It is entirely a matter for the producer's taste and sense of fitness. One thing is certain, anything of this kind must be done so subtly and unobtrusively that the spectator does not consciously notice it. If the dimming is obvious he will begin to ask himself: "Is it supposed to be growing dark? No, the afternoon light is still strong outside the window. What's happening?" By this time, he is no longer with you, and the actors have to fight to get him back again.

When in doubt about "emotional" lighting, in a serious realistic play, don't use it.

In the same way avoid bringing up special lighting on an actor who has a long important speech or has to be noticed suddenly after lurking in a corner. Shift the actor into the stronger light that is there already; this is another good reason for thinking out lighting while you are planning your moves.

Thrillers and Melodramas

These may have naturalistic settings, but they are fairly far removed from life as we know it, and an audience is prepared for exciting effects of contrast and emphasis. In fact, the more absurd the plot and characterization, the more justified you are in spotting the villain with magenta or green, or in blacking out everything except one strong beam which shows Dr. Jekyll becoming Mr. Hyde. But don't do it in such plays as Sartre's In Camera, for the horror is in the situation and dialogue and needs no underlining from the switchboard.

REALISTIC EXTERIORS

Here the chief thing is the sky, but as its lighting has been dealt with previously, I shall only add a word of warning to those lucky people who have powerful sky-cloth units. See that your actors are lit as strongly as your sky. Silhouette is very effective for short periods, but the spectator soon tires of a bright sky against which dark, faceless figures move and speak. For most of you, however, the problem is to get any sky-cloth lighting at all.

On the main acting area, your light should have some relation to its source. Decide from which direction the sun is supposed to be coming and use the same technique as for indoor motivated light—more and brighter from that angle, using both spots and floods. A good direction is from one or other of the perches (inside the corners of the proscenium) as it is often difficult to fit lights to shine from high up in the wings and from directly down-stage is too easy and uninteresting.

Floods are rather more important than spots in daylight scenes, and should be arranged first, spots being brought in gently on the areas where important action is to take place. Colours should be white (open floods or spots), straw, lavender, steel, gold, deepening to pale pink for evening, but *not* heavy amber.

Take every opportunity to have shadows cast by scenery such as houses, trees, bushes, walls, arches, but, since most stage lighting has to come from the front, it is not easy to make shadows that can be seen by the audience; strong side-lighting is necessary.

There is nothing more satisfying to a lighting artist than a fine blue sky, with an interesting groundrow of distant landscape in front, some walls and roofs, and figures moving about with faces lit so as to stand out in contrast to the sky. Shaw's plays, unlike most, give many opportunities, as in *Captain Brassbound's Conversion*, or *Caesar and Cleopatra*, or *Man and Superman*, and when your stage is well equipped, you should welcome the chance to get away from "one interior throughout."

NON-REALISTIC

Under this clumsy title I include plays where time, place and mood are changed while the curtain is up, often in a multiple set. Examples are Priestley's *Johnson Over Jordan*; *Top of The Ladder* by Tyrone Guthrie; Arthur Miller's *Death of a Salesman*; and *The Glass Menagerie* and several others by Tennessee Williams; all plays that are a joy to an imaginative producer and are almost impossible to stage without good lighting.

In these, delicate touches are rarely necessary. Each scene is so short that the illumination must make an immediate and telling impact—tender, nightmarish, serene, harsh, exciting, sensual—and you can use any device that will do the job. A colour-wheel, which brings round six or seven different gelatines in front of a spot lens, is very effective if revolved rapidly during, perhaps, a scene of screaming hysterics; the following spot, never employed in normal plays but common in the variety theatre, can be horrifying if used implacably to chase a man stricken by conscience and remorse; the solitary baby spot from the footlights will throw weird light on the face of a man in mental agony.

Much careful rehearsal and positioning of lights is essential in this kind of production, and Joe may find he needs one or two assistants to help him with complicated dimming and switching. You had better warn your committee also in good time that some supplementary spots may have to be hired to cover all the acting areas. A sitting-room may appear twice in one act, once in the clear light of morning, and once in the late evening. A single spot may not do, as it is unlikely that Joe will be able to change the gelatine from steel to pink while the curtain is up, you will almost certainly have to use two spots. On the other hand you may decide that a change of colour is unnecessarily fussy, and compromise on a gold-tint for both.

SHAKESPEARE

Many of the foregoing remarks apply, but remember that Shakespeare wrote for daylight performance, and his words need little help in the creation of atmosphere. Here and there, as in the heath scenes of *Macbeth*, you can use contrast and colour to heighten his effect, but for most of his plays you would be wise to avoid anything startling.

9

From Script to Light-plot

I HAVE said once or twice in this book that you must think out your lighting while preparing your production, and now I hope to show how it is done. I shall assume that you have a reasonably good lighting-set, some idea of what its various units can do, and a clear understanding of the aims described in Chapter 2. Even if your set is inadequate, I think you will learn something from what follows. Much of it may seem hopelessly idealistic, only possible with elaborate apparatus, but keep the principles in mind and carry out as many of them as you can.

LIGHT-PLOT FOR AN INTERIOR SCENE

I have imagined a serious one-act play, obscurely titled, in the fashion of the moment, *Tomorrow Was Yesterday*. The scene is a sitting-room, and you at once cut down the author's lavish furnishings to a minimum of—

Sofa LC
Table RC with three chairs
Arm-chair UC
Small coffee table DC with chair.

Your reading informs you that action takes place, in order of importance—

Centre-stage
At table R
On Sofa
At arch R
Round arm-chair
At small table.

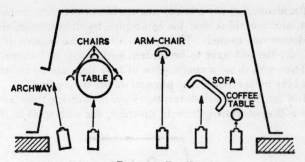

FIG. 7. A METHOD OF SPOTTING

A dull way of spotting five acting areas.

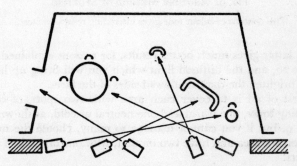

Fig. 8. ANOTHER METHOD OF SPOTTING

Much more interesting modelling is got by angling spot beams across stage. Floods or battens will take care of the dark sides of faces.

Spots

Remembering my advice, you decide to get these areas lit first, and you think that Joe can scrape together enough spots to devote one to each. If not, then areas at the bottom of the priority list will have to be content with floods or battens.

Then you draw a rough plan of how they are to be used, but here inexperience may put you on the wrong lines.

In Figs. 7 and 8 are shown two ways of covering these areas, one with spots staring straight up-stage, one with spots angled.

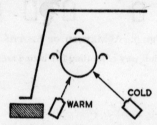

FIG. 9. ANOTHER METHOD OF SPOTTING

This contrast of colour tone gives interesting results on faces.

The latter gives much better results, for reasons explained on page 26, and the diffused light which you will bring up later will brighten the dark shadowed sides of the faces.

Best of all is to cover each area with two spots, of contrasting tones, one warm and one neutral or cold, as shown in Fig. 9, but if you cannot manage so many, choose the most important area and have two on that, with one on each of the others.

Centre-stage, strangely enough, often needs no special lighting, for with so many beams crossing it, an actor's face can hardly avoid being well lit, but of course, if in practice you find there is a dark patch in the middle, you must hasten to remedy that, even at the expense of other places.

F.O.H. spots are treated in the same way, as suggested in Fig. 10. In some halls, the F.O.H. are so difficult to get at that their direction and colour must remain fixed. They usually point straight at the stage and carry amber gelatines, and if such a misfortune is likely to spoil your picture, either do

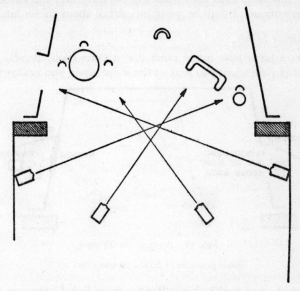

FIG. 10. ANOTHER METHOD OF SPOTTING

Suggested arrangement of four spots as F.O.H.

without them or have them dimmed till they are harmless, yet of some help.

Floods

I need not say much about diffused lighting, as this exists on every stage and is easy enough to plan. On a medium-sized stage, say 18 ft × 14 ft, one 500-watt flood will supply most of the general illumination required, though two at 250 watts give more variety of colour and direction. If you have only one, hang it a little off-centre in No. 1 bar and angle it slightly towards the middle of the stage; if you have two, position and angle them as shown in Fig. 11.

Batten-light cannot be changed in direction, only in colour and intensity, so in your planning you have only the former to worry about. I shall be going into detail about colour later.

Off-stage Lights

You have now made notes about your spots, floods, and F.O.H., but when you look at the script again you realize that

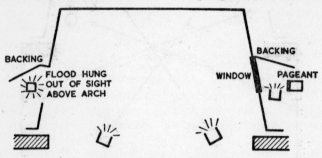

FIG. 11. ANGLES OF FLOODS

Some positions of floods, on-stage and off.

our unknown author has called for more lights. He says that it is about 6 p.m. mid-April, cloudy outside. Soon after the rise, the sun comes out for a few minutes and shines through the window left. Then it goes in again and dusk falls. There is another window up-stage showing the sky. All this is mentioned in the lines so I shall take it that you don't mean to cut out these references but to give the audience full value.

Your notes will now include: "Pageant (or flood) through window L. Flood on window backing. Sky-cloth batten."

The window backing reminds you of another, behind the arch. So another note: "Flood on arch backing, 7 ft or 8 ft up." Why the last bit? Because if it is lower, it will throw advance shadows of actors about to enter. The floods can be seen in Fig. 11, and the batten in Fig. 12.

Odds

Coming back to the room itself you add: "Small flood through fireplace down R, lamp on table R, standard lamp up L. Wall brackets each side of up-stage window and above fireplace," and any other refinements you care to devise.

It is worth noting that all the units mentioned are either hung high up or standing at floor level. You should concentrate on the former (spots, floods and battens) when you are planning, as it is those that Joe will want to know about first so that he can get them set for your lighting rehearsal and clear his ladders away. The units on stage level (sunlight, backing, floods, fire, etc.), can be altered much more easily at short notice, without stopping rehearsal.

Colour

In Chapter 7 when dealing with conventions, I said it was a concession to realism to motivate your light, that is, give it colour and direction that will correspond to the supposed source.

Here is your chance to try it out. The author has stipulated sunshine through a window, left, a fire, right, and artificial light from brackets, table-lamp and standard-lamp. You need not worry about the latter since it is there mainly as decoration and nobody does any acting up in that corner, but the others at once suggest cold tints for the units that point across from window side to arch side, and warm tints for those that point from the fire and the table-lamp. So the tones in the five spots in Fig. 8 will be reading from *our* left, warm, neutral, cold, cold. As the up-stage window throws its light mostly on people's backs, we disregard it in this connexion.

The same applies to the floods, but battens, which are not directional, had better have one circuit cold and one warm, with the third anything you fancy.

The off-stage lights are coloured according to the job they do. The pageant, which represents late sunshine, has gold or rose or salmon (not amber); the window-backing flood white or pale blue, the sky-cloth batten one circuit of light blue for day sky and two of darker blue for night sky, the arch backing flood which is supposed to reflect artificial light from a passage, one of the warm colours, the fire as indicated on page 40.

If you have all the equipment needed, your final layout will be something like the one shown in Fig. 12.

Dimming

When the curtain goes up, you cannot have everything on at full strength, because the sun is supposed to come out for a while later on. Therefore, your opening light must be checked (dimmed) so that the warm units are full on, but the pageant and the cold lights indoors are able to come up a bit when a character says: "I believe the sun's coming out." As the clouds come over again, the process is reversed, and as dusk falls the dimmers bring down the pageant, the window backing, the sky-cloth batten and the cold indoor lights. When the room lights are supposed to be switched on, the brackets leap into life, the cold lights (nearly out by now) are brought up quickly to quarter, or half, and the standard-lamp and table-lamp are turned on by actors. As the latter lights up, the spot trained on the table is switched on at the same moment.

If you have only one spot per acting area, you will have the difficult job of deciding which are to be warm indoor and which cold "auxiliary sunshine" with cold floods or battens. In fact, with some lighting-sets I have had to operate, only about one-tenth of the above recommendations could be carried out! Don't despair, however, if yours is like that; money is well spent on hiring as a temporary measure.

LIGHT-PLOT FOR AN EXTERIOR SCENE

I have invented another one-act play, *Today Is The Day After*, with more going on by way of lighting than in any real one I know. The setting is a house-front left with door, a well centre, a tree up right, a range of mountains at the back. The plan is shown in Fig. 13.

Acting areas are round the objects mentioned above, and to

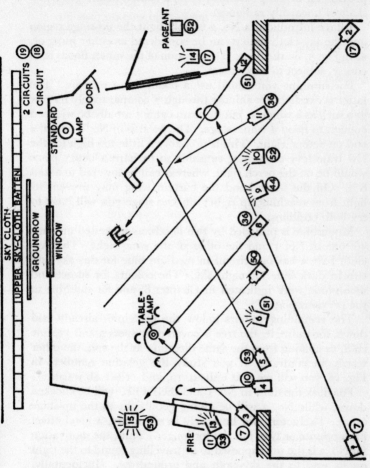

Fig. 12. Lighting Layout for Interior Scene

Lighting layout for a conventional box-set. Gelatine numbers are circled.

a lesser extent up left in front of the groundrow. We have to provide for evening sunshine, dusk, a sunset, moonlight and a shaft of unearthly radiance.

I have introduced a No. 2 to help light the up-stage region and the sky-cloth batten can be considered as either hung or, as in Fig. 5, on the floor. The position of the sunset floods is, of course, subject to experiment.

For sunshine you should use a flood, not a pageant. The latter is excellent for shining through a comparatively narrow gap such as a window, but its beam cannot usually be widened enough to flood a whole stage. The flood is in No. 1 near the end on actors' right. This is probably a little too high for the low trajectory of evening sunshine so perhaps a better place would be on the perch right, where it can be lowered to about 8 ft. On the other hand the curtain wing may prevent its light from reaching up right; on *your* stage you will have to try both positions.

Moonshine is provided by two floods, as suggested on page 39, one in No. 1 and the other in the wing right. The sky-cloth batten has one circuit in medium blue for day sky and two in dark blue for night sky. The colours for sunset and moonshine were indicated in Chapter 8, and for sunshine in the previous play.

The remaining colours follow the principles already laid down, for example, the tree is covered by spots 5 and 11, one cold, as coming from the same direction as the sun, the other warm, in contrast. If you study the gelatine numbers in Fig. 13, you will see that units 9, 10, and 11 are all warm.

For dusk the units in No. 1 and the F.O.H. will be checked down, while No. 2 will be giving good light to the up-stage areas. The actors will be nearly in silhouette, a good effect for a minute or two, but not for longer. Thus, the motivation for No. 2 is the sun supposed to be travelling round to the right on its way to the sky-cloth and groundrow. (Incidentally, when I had finished my first rough sketch for Fig. 13, I found that I had put the sunset up-stage left. My sun had either gone right round and across the sky-cloth unperceived, or had

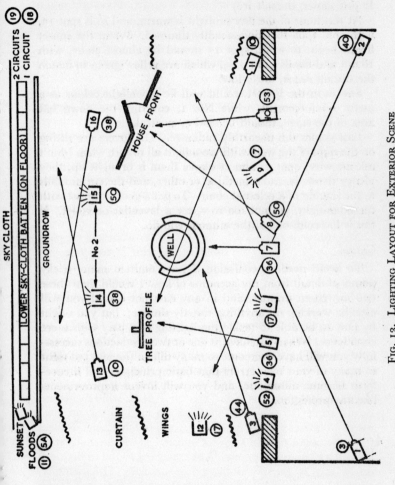

FIG. 13. LIGHTING LAYOUT FOR EXTERIOR SCENE
Gelatine numbers are circled.

tired of its normal course and retreated counter-clockwise. It just shows, doesn't it?)

At this hour of the day sunlight is warm, and so is spot 13, with cold spot 16 being steadily dimmed. When the sunset floods begin to work, spot 13 should be almost alone, with 16 out and floods 14 and 15, which are yellow-green to match the distant scene, fairly low.

Spot 2 in the F.O.H. could well be moonlight colour as a useful reinforcement, while No. 1, covering the down left area of the stage, should be cold or neutral.

Last comes the unearthly radiance. The lovers are sitting on the steps of the well, with moonlight all round, when (don't ask me why) spot 7, almost above them is brought up, they pledge themselves to something or other, and the curtain falls to the singing of a celestial choir. To get a good contrast with the moonlight, yet not too rosy, try a lavender or violet. If this is too cold, one of the salmons will do.

General

To avoid needless confusion, I have omitted many tricky points of detail from my accounts of how I would light these two unwritten dramas, and in any case not one of you will ever be working on anything exactly similar; but you ought by now to be able to tackle the lighting of a play with more confidence. When you have lit one or two productions successfully you will have overcome so many difficulties and put right so many of your own errors that basic principles will thenceforth become automatic, and you will invent improvements like any professional.

10

Working with Your Electrician

OUR imaginary Joe may be anyone from a youth who can just do simple wiring and work the dimmers without blowing too many fuses, to a fully qualified electrician who can read a play and work out a lighting scheme of great beauty and interpretative value. In many years of messing about on amateur stages I have met only one of the latter quality, and he is in immense demand all over his district. But even he, being at work all day, prefers to be given a clear idea of what the producer is aiming at. He can usually improve on it before the dress rehearsal, but he has no time to think it all out from the beginning.

So I shall take an average Joe, and try to help you to get his confidence and willing co-operation. Each of you will have to work out your own plan for dealing with the temperament, vanity, obstructiveness, obtuseness, inertia, and plain cussedness that some electricians are prone to, but, assuming that you have him on your side, how can you make things clear and easy for him?

Vague waffling about the artistic effect you want is quite useless. Get things down on paper, and here are two schemes that will form a useful basis. See that Joe has them at least a week before the dress rehearsal, preferably a fortnight, as he needs time to cut his gelatines and do rewiring, and repositioning.

LIGHTING LAYOUT

When you began to work on the script, you made a diagram of your stage, with the scenery you would like and the furniture, and the exits. For your lighting layout you should do another, with all the lighting units shown in plan. You may need some help from Joe here, and of course if you cannot get near the stage at all, you may have to ask for a plan to be sent to you. Detail in setting and furniture is not required; the essential thing is to indicate clearly how you want each unit to be directed and what colours you want for the gelatines.

If you have read Chapter 8, you will have referred once or twice to Figs. 12 and 13, which are the layouts for the two imaginary plays. These plans, however, could be for Acts I and II of a full-length play—many of Shaw's change from interior to exterior—but if you compare the drawings you will notice that most of the units are in different places and differently angled and coloured. In practice, you would be giving Joe and his staff a lot of trouble during the first interval, especially if he has only one pair of steps on which to reach No. 1. Ask him about this before you make violent changes between acts. Altering angles and gelatines may not be a great task, but shifting units is.

You may also notice that the two F.O.H. for the exterior scene (Fig. 13) have been angled farther down-stage. This is to avoid actors' shadows being thrown on the sky-cloth. A problem arises here if an exterior follows an interior, as the F.O.H. angle that would be harmless for the latter may be fatal to the former. It is quite improper for someone to come out and readjust F.O.H. during the interval of a performance, so, if you have not enough spots to keep two for Act I and two others for Act II, you must angle them for the Act II exterior off the sky-cloth. Bad luck on Act I but there it is.

Another matter on which Joe may be very firm is that he has not enough dimmers of the correct rating to control each circuit separately. He will, therefore, have to link some units in pairs, and as this needs tedious wiring, find out about it before you finish your layout. It is an annoying complication, but it is something Joe may be unable to avoid until the committee votes him more money.

There is one thing you can do, however, which will please him. If there is a unit which is on all the time and is undimmed, say so on your layout. Joe may be hard pressed to find enough circuits to cover everything, and would be glad to be able to run the fire flood in Fig. 12 from a point somewhere backstage not connected with the switchboard. Also, if units are switched off or on but never dimmed, such as table- or standard-lamps, add those, as he may have a couple of circuits on his board that can't be connected to any dimmer.

OPERATIONS PLOT

This is the list of directions, showing what you want Joe to do throughout the performance, and since many variations of it are possible, it is rather difficult to describe. The simplest way is probably to write your instructions in the margins of a copy of the play, underlining the cue words. But this, as any librarian will tell you, is most undesirable. Further, even if the copy is your own, the margins may be so small that your writing will be too cramped for Joe to read in his weak pilot light, especially when he is reaching for dimmers or switches at the other end of the board.

I prefer to write my instructions in fairly large thick capitals on foolscap sheets, starting each new act on a new page. One thing to be remembered is that Joe will be able to hear loud noises such as a shot or a cheer but may miss a line of quiet dialogue, and that he can often see only a small part of the acting area. You will have to arrange signals from the Stage Manager when sounds are low or when the cue is some movement by an actor, and write, "on signal from S.M." on the sheet.

You ought not to need to open your Operations Plot with a description of direction or colour—that should be cared for by the Lighting Layout—but Joe will need to know what is on or off and what intensities you want.

So it starts—

ACT I

Evening, about 6 p.m. mid-April, cloudy outside.
At rise, FULL ON Spots 1, 4, 5, 7, 12
Flood 10

CHECKED TO HALF Spots 2, 8, 11
Floods 9, 14
Pageant
Sky-cloth Batten (3 cir-
cuits)

OFF
Spot 3
Flood 6

The half-strength of the cold units and the outside lights is to allow for the operation of bringing up the sunshine and its auxiliary indoor light. Spot 3, warm, will come up when the table-lamp is lit, and Flood 6, warm, when the room lights are switched on.

The next item si not essential, but it helps Joe's work. I like to mark his copy of the play (and you can't expect him to take an intelligent interest if he hasn't one) with large figures in light erasable pencil in the margin, each one corresponding to a switchboard operation described on the sheet, so that, having set his lights for the rise of the curtain, he sees from his script that his next job is half-way down page 3. On the sheet it reads—

CUE 1, p. 3. At line "I believe the sun's coming out," or signal from S.M. bring up to full Pageant, Spots 2, 8, 11, Floods 9 and 14, Sky-cloth Batten (all circuits).

Then, near the end of the act, when indoor lighting has been established, someone may switch off all the room lights, but there is still some light out of doors, and you might write—

CUE 5, p. 28. At S.M.'s signal, *black-out* except lights outside set LC, Pageant, Floods 13, 14, 15, and Sky-cloth Batten.

This kind of blackout may give Joe a good deal of trouble, as many boards have no arrangements for putting certain circuits on a blackout master-switch and leaving others unaffected. He may have to experiment with all sorts of devices to get it right, so, once more, warn him early.

Later on in the play, say, in Act II, he might find this—

CUE 9, p. 41. At S.M.'s signal start seven-minute check

of Sky-cloth Batten light-blue circuits, Pageant, Spots 1, 3, 5, 10, 11. Flood 4. All these down to a quarter by about foot of p. 46.

CUE 10, p. 43. At "Get out and stay out!" bring up sunset floods over five minutes and check Spot 8 and Flood 4 to half over one minute.

and so on through all the business of dusk, sunset, fading of sunset, moonrise.

Remember that if you say only "Check," or "Bring up," Joe will run his dimmer straight down or up; tell him how much you want each light to be increased or decreased, and over how long a period. Also, if you ask him to do two simultaneous operations lasting different times, as in Cues 9 and 10, he may need an assistant.

As I have already pointed out, there is no end to the different ways of drawing up an Operations Plot, but they must all give Joe a clear conception of—

1. Where each cue comes in the script.

2. Whether he is to follow the script and get his cue from it, or depend on the Stage Manager. The final decision need not be your responsibility—Joe and the S.M. are perfectly capable of working it out quickly during rehearsal. S.M. will then mark his own copy: "Cue to lights," or something similar.

3. Which units are involved. You must have an agreed system of numbering and/or describing.

4. To what fraction of full light you want any unit checked or brought up. (Don't worry about what position the dimmer is in, as Joe may find that half-strength of light is got by moving the slide only one-quarter up from OUT. Leave him to sort out all that for himself.)

5. For how long you want the alteration of light to go on, expressed either in minutes or script page numbers. Both are used in Cue 9.

6. Any changes of colour or direction that you want him to effect during intervals. But remember my warning about not asking too much.

These two pieces of paper-work, the Lighting Layout and the Operations Plot, may seem to be laborious jobs, but the saving of time and temper at your final rehearsals will convince you that they are worth doing. And what is more important, you will find that Joe has got everything ready for you and is rarin' to go, proud to show how well he can work from clear instructions. He will, of course, be prepared for modifications when some of your bright ideas don't work in practice, but that is vastly different from the usual waiting about while this, that and the other are tried out, with the actors wondering about the last bus home and rapidly losing faith in your powers of organization.

11

Lighting Rehearsal

THIS chapter will be almost useless to those luckless producers who cannot get on to the stage till the day of the only dress rehearsal and whose electrician is not at liberty to do his practical preparations till about six o'clock on the same evening. The plans and lists described in the previous chapter will be of some help, but they envisage a situation in which Joe can do a part of the work beforehand, and I can do little but commiserate with a producer trying to get a complicated lighting plot into operation between six and half past seven. If you know, when choosing the play, that the lighting will be difficult and that the stage will be in continuous use by others up to your dress rehearsal, there is no sense in attempting the impossible—you will have either to simplify your lighting ideas or choose another play.

On the assumption, however, that Joe has been able to get at the job and that you have an hour or two to spend on nothing but lighting, here is how to make the best of that time.

Make sure that at least two assistants have been laid on— one for Joe and one for you. Their functions will become apparent shortly. Get the furniture (or substitutes for it) arranged exactly as it will be in the show and as much of the setting as possible, particularly sky-cloth, windows, fireplace, doors and their backings put up. Check over the gelatines which have (you hope) been already inserted in each unit and you are ready to set the spots in No. 1 (I shall use the layout in Fig. 12 as my example).

Get Joe to switch on Spot 3, and adjust it so that it covers the table and the chairs round it. (Here is where his assistant comes in, as someone must switch on and off while the other nips up a step-ladder and moves the lantern.) If the edge of

65

the circle or ellipse is too hard, have a frosted gelatine put in. Seat *your* assistant in one chair after another and make sure he is lit. It is now up to you to decide whether to have Spot 8 dealt with now, as it also lights the table, or let it wait its turn. The former means a longer move for the step-ladder, and you can always have Spot 3 put on again when you arrive at Spot 8, so let's go on to Spot 4. Same process again, with your helper moving about in front of the fireplace and sitting in the chair. (Tell him, by the way, not to keep looking up into the spots—it's bad for the eyes.) You settle Spot 8 when you come to it and then have Spot 3 on as well to see how the colours blend and the shadows fall, and of course you do the same for Spots 11 and 5. When you have fixed the last one, Spot 12, test the F.O.H., first singly, then together, ensuring that no light shines anywhere on the proscenium or on the front rows of audience, and that they are doing their job of illuminating the actor who comes down-stage beyond the effective reach of the units in No. 1.

You then pass on to the diffused lighting from Floods 6, 9, 10. Try each one alone first, watching the edge of the light to see that it is not a sharp line (frosts again, probably) and that it covers the required area. Then, of course, have them all on together. Next, cut them and put on all the spots, including F.O.H. Now bring the floods up again until the balance is right, not too patchy, not too flat, and the main part of the job is done. For an exterior scene, it is usually better to start with the floods, as they are often more important than the spots.

Try in turn the footlights, pageant, the backing-lights, the fireplace, the sky-cloth batten, noting such points as unwanted spill of light from any of these outside units; shadows of actors about to enter being cast on backings; bulbs in standard- and table-lamps too strong, or so weak as to be killed and made pointless when the main lighting is on; elimination of stray reflections from mirrors and glass-fronted pictures; general tidiness.

Take as long as you can spare to gaze at the final result,

asking your assistant to move about so that you can see whether the units blend smoothly or whether he appears to be walking past a lighted train—bright and dim alternately. When he is in the main acting area, does he stand out against his background, or is the scenery too brilliantly flooded? Does he throw shadows on the sky-cloth in an open-air scene? Does he block off the sunshine through the window because the pageant lantern is too low? If he is in semi-darkness up left does that matter? Is any actor going to be important there?

When you are reasonably satisfied, take Joe through all the dimming changes. You probably cannot spend eight or ten minutes on one slow check—that can wait till the dress rehearsal—but you can call out the cues from your duplicate copy and make sure that your Operations Plot really works. It is seldom a hundred per cent, and you must always make sure it is not your fault before pointing out any error.

Finally, be very patient with Joe when you ask for an alteration. Sometimes he can do it in a few seconds, but at other times he and his crew appear to have gone into a coma. They haven't, of course, they are figuring out how to do your will without upsetting everything else, but a gentle inquiry: "Could that be done later?" will often get things moving again. Then, when any arrangement of lights is just as you want it, ask Joe to come out and look at it with you from the front. This will not only give him the feeling that he is a clever chap, but will go far towards fitting him to take over the lighting of a play if some other producer won't or can't do it.

12

Festival Lighting

No adjudicator who has been through the amateur mill will ever reprove a team for bad lighting without knowing what the conditions back-stage are, what the lighting-set is capable of, and what sort of electrician is in charge. If, however, these are all of a high standard he can justifiably say: "I don't think the producer made as good a shot at the lighting as he could have done. Even in Festival conditions he could have had a spot . . ." How mortifying for a producer to have to agree!

Festival lighting-sets (and the men in charge) vary enormously. Some sets are so inflexible and ponderous that changes from one play to another are extremely difficult to make in the allotted time, and every play has to have the same gelatine colours, and the same positions and angles of units. All that can be varied is the dimming and the number of units switched on. In such cases, Bill[1] gathers in all the light plots from all the producers, works out the arrangements that will give everybody something, and operates his board as well as he can for each play. That, if not artistic, is at least fair.

Another variation is the amount of time you can spend beforehand studying the stage and talking to Bill. It may be only a few minutes, so here are some priorities to help you to make the best of a brief encounter. I am assuming you have a fairly difficult job of lighting to do.

Things to look for on your own. How much concentrated light (spots, etc.) and how much diffused light? How many F.O.H.? Are they in front, or at the sides, or both? Are there dips for your windows and backing lights? How is the sky-cloth lit, from above, below or both?

[1] Note change of name. He is not your Joe, alas.

Make rapid notes and sketches, for you may have to re-design your Lighting Layout completely.

Things to ask Bill. Can he change colours and redirect units between plays? Has he a separate dimmer for each circuit, or must there be a lot of linking? Has he stage-level floods (if you haven't seen any) for your off-stage lighting? Can he do a partial blackout? Will his F.O.H. gelatines, and any other unchangeables, be dark or pale colours? How does he like his cues, from book, sheet or your S.M.?

If your Layout and Operations Plot are already reasonably operable on Bill's set, give them to him at once. If not, take them home and adapt them. But whatever you do, make sure he understands the priorities of your play—that for instance it is essential to have a 42 Pale Violet spot on a chair left-centre switched on after a five-second blackout, as much of the play's effect depends on this. You would like moonlight streaming through a window right, but this is less vital. If he can give you a pool of warm light round a table-lamp so much the better, but it is not important.

From this, Bill will be able to concentrate on that spot left-centre, and it will comfort you to hear him say, "I can promise you that, and I'll do my best for the others." It is certainly unfair on any harassed Festival electrician that he should be asked to fuss over comparative trifles.

When preparing your instructions, try to put yourself in his place. Keep asking: "Is this perfectly clear? Can he be expected to do these two things at the same time?" You have probably worked it all out with Joe at rehearsal and he knows it backwards, but it is completely new to Bill and he has two or three other plays to cope with that evening.

It would probably save you hours of work and worry if you could bring Joe with you on the night and put him on the board. Obviously you will have to be very tactful about it—perhaps preliminary soundings should go through the Festival Stage Manager—but do not be surprised if you get a firm negative. Switchboards can be ruined by inexpert handling, and most Bills prefer to do the whole job themselves. Only if Joe has worked with Bill on the board is Bill likely to agree. There is of course no reason why you should not take Joe with you on the preliminary visit to help state your wishes for you.

In the melancholy event of your not being able to see the set and its Bill, send him clear plans, with demands reduced to the minimum, your priorities clearly stated as above, a copy of the play and an Operations Plot. Then pray that he is as good as Joe.

13

Lighting for Plays in Churches

BY

THE REV. P. BULLOCK-FLINT

of

St. Mary Magdalen Church, Tilehurst, Reading

YOU are going to do a Nativity or Passion Play in the church this year, and it is almost certain that someone in authority has said: "It must not be 'theatrical'." You fully agree, for the only reason for doing the play in church is that it is an act of worship; the church must be used as a church, and not turned into a theatre by building a stage over the choir stalls and rigging a front curtain, backcloth and No. 1 batten. If your play needs these theatrical devices, please go back into the hall where you already have them, and where they do not interfere with the normal use of the church.

A Religious play is to the glory of God, so it must be the best that we are capable of, in acting, costumes, lighting and make-up. A swathing of bedspreads and the old front-room curtains, cotton-wool whiskers and a couple of biscuit-tin floods on the front pew are downright bad religion, since they are bad theatre and so not worthy of being offered to God. Nor will the remark that it is "nothing ambitious, just a little Nativity Play," excuse careless inartistic lighting.

AIMS

Assuming then that you have a play which will benefit from being performed in church, how are you to set about lighting it? First, turn back to Chapter 2 and have another look at the aims of good stage lighting. They all apply to work in church, especially the first. A church is usually much bigger than a hall, and the lanterns have to be placed farther from the actors; you will, therefore, need more light if the audience is to see them. This applies particularly to night scenes. People have come to *see* your play, so it is useless to have the shepherds revealed in the glow of an electric torch covered in red paper to represent firelight. Nor will the lights used on Sundays for the choir be adequate; they are designed to light hymn-books, and you want to light the faces of the actors, not just the tops of their heads.

In addition to the aims listed in Chapter 2, there are three special aims in church plays. (They are not arranged here in order of importance.)

(*a*) To eliminate distracting features, such as gilded organ pipes or marble and slate memorial tablets. You could hang a piece of curtain over the offending objects, but that would be crude and obvious. It is much better to keep all light for the acting areas and for helpful pieces of architecture, leaving the rest in darkness; how this can be done is explained later.

(*b*) To enhance the idea. Many of the plays now being performed in churches are of the stylized type in which, though there are some localized scenes, the principal part of the play is where the chorus comment on the events and their significance. One is really lighting an idea rather than a scene.

(*c*) To suggest time and place. In church you will have no scenery, so the difference between Herod's palace and the top of Mount Calvary can be indicated only by light, words and a few props. The principles of lighting from an assumed source (Chapters 8 and 9) will be helpful here. Differences of time are best suggested by variations of colour, rather than by merely reducing the intensity of the light. Thus, the Shepherds' scene would be better lit in deep blue, with a shaft of moonlight picking out the actors.

COLOUR

Because of the lack of realistic backgrounds, colour is considerably more important in church than on stage. Different colours rouse different emotions. Blue is hard and harsh;

red is sympathetic, even amusing; yellow suggests evil, sensuality or impending doom, and so on. This is the basic principle to observe when working out the lighting colour scheme for a stylized play, but now turn back again to Chapter 2. The last aim on the list, unobtrusiveness, should be moved up into second place. Almost all your play is going to be lit with this in mind, and you will not achieve "subtle help in creation of mood" if you stun your audience with garish colours suddenly flashed on. You will need the paler tints derived from the basic colours gently faded in as the text of the play requires them. Below is a list of gelatine shades classified in a different way from that shown on page 35.

Sympathetic		Unsympathetic		Harsh	
Pale Lavender	36	Pale Yellow	50	Steel Blue	17
Gold Tint	51	Light Amber	2	Light Blue	18
Pale Gold	52	Canary	49	Pale Blue	40
Pale Salmon	53	Pea Green	21		
Pale Rose	54				
Light Salmon	9				
Deep Salmon	8				

Neutral-sympathetic		Neutral-unsympathetic		Neutral-harsh	
Straw	3	Chocolate Tint	55	Pale Grey	60
		Pale Chocolate	56		

What we are trying to do is to light the general playing area to suggest the time and place of the action, while highlighting particular groups of actors in colours to suit the mood of their lines. For instance, it may be night time outside the inn at Bethlehem (general light Dark Blue 19). The innkeeper appears in a shaft of moonlight (Steel Blue 17, harsh) which does away with the need for a property door, while Mary and Joseph catch a glow of 36 or 54, both sympathetic colours, one of which (36) has a touch of blue in it to blend in with the general idea of night. Alternatively, it may be noon on Calvary, with the soldiers and crowd in a hot sultry unsympathetic tint (2 or 3), and the priests, spotted with 21, marked out as still more hostile than the crowd. Mary, John and Mary Magdalen at the foot of the Cross, however, are high-lighted in 53 or 54 or even 8. When the darkness comes and all lights are dimmed, to nearly out, the yellowish tints in the general lighting will be strengthened by the reddish glow of the lamp filaments, suggesting the evil of the surrounding world, but the Cross will stand out in a sympathetic light.

When you have set up the colours suggested in these examples, and Joe switches everything on full, you may be horrified by the patchiness of the result. The answer is to adjust the dimmers so that the spots are not so strong and the general lighting stronger. When the right balance is achieved, Mary and Joseph will not stand out in a blob of pink with the priests in a pool of yellowy-green and nothing lit between them; there will be a gentle gradation from one group to the next. (Do not forget to give Joe some chance to get his settings right *before* the night of your one and only dress rehearsal.)

APPARATUS

I have been writing glibly about pools of light and about balancing dimmers, so this seems the place to stop and think about the type, position and control of the lanterns.

It has already been emphasized that light must be con-centrated on the playing area only, to divert attention from distracting architecture and ornament. This means that ordinary floods and battens are useless, though a narrow-angle flood (Fig. 2c) can be used in some churches. Since we require pools of light often measuring 12–18 ft across, not little hard discs, there is no point in using mirror spots (Fig. 1c), and even the standard spot (Fig. 1a) can often give too narrow a beam. When this type is all I can get, I frequently use it with the lens removed.

I have found that the most satisfactory lanterns are home-made, consisting of a large round tin which will vary from 8 in. to 12 in. in depth according to the amount of concentra-tion required, and fitted with a slide to take gelatines. The light is supplied by the kind of bulb used in shop-window lighting, known as a "reflector floodlight." It is also called a "spotlight" by retailers, so make sure you get a mushroom-shaped lamp with its own reflector inside and a longish neck; 150 watts seems to be the maximum power. These lanterns have the advantage of giving a fairly generous beam of

light with a concentrated spot in the centre; they are not heavy, which makes them easy to mount; they are economical in wattage and you can use lamps of lower power; they are cheap, so you can have a lot of them. The disadvantages are that the spread of the beam can be scarcely ad-justed at all, and if they have to be situated a long way from the playing area their light spreads so wide that you are better with common spotlights. They are so light in weight, however, that they can usually be set up on wooden towers placed between pews close to the acting area. In many ways,

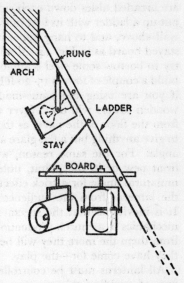

FIG. 14. HANGING LANTERNS IN CHURCH

square biscuit-tins are easier to adapt and suspend, but they are liable to throw straight edges of shadow across fluted pillars and other irregular features; I have found that circular edges are much less noticeable. Three aspects of this type of unit are shown in Fig. 14.

The principles of positioning the lanterns have already been discussed in Chapter 5, and if you think of all lanterns as being F.O.H. spots you can look round for places which will give the correct angle. If your church has side galleries or iron tie-bars in the roof, your problems are solved (though Joe may need to be a bit of a monkey—fortunately most Joes are). If there are tall pillars down each side of the nave, a well-padded board fitted with brackets can be tied to the pillar and the lanterns hung from that. Make sure, however, that the pillars are tall enough, in most churches they are not. If there are arcaded aisles down each side, it is sometimes possible to put up a ladder with its foot in the aisle and its top against the wall above, and to hang apparatus from the rungs or from a stayed board as in Fig. 14. If none of these devices will work, try to borrow some steel scaffolding from a local builder and build a couple of towers 15–20 ft high at either side of the nave; if you are using the home-made lanterns described above, wooden towers will do. Never use telescopic lighting stands from the floor of the nave, as they cannot reach high enough to give anything but a flat glare at face level, the worst possible angle. For the same reason, avoid putting lanterns in the front pew or in the pulpit, unless you particularly want an unnatural angle for a trick effect. Whenever you can, screen the lanterns from the audience with a piece of hardboard. It is inevitable that the spectators will see something of the mechanics in a church production, but the more you can hide from them the more they will be able to concentrate on what they have come for—the play.

All lanterns must be controlled by dimmers. There is no way of avoiding this expense, since the whole lighting-plot must be an affair of gradual changes and cross-fading, with hardly any switching on and off. The best thing is to hire a board from a stage-lighting firm (*see* page 80). Tell them how many lanterns you will be using and whether any of them will be linked to work on the same circuit and so need only one dimmer to control each group; they will then know what size of board to send you. Place it in such a position that Joe can both see and hear what is happening without being seen. That may be the west gallery, or a transept, or behind a pillar, or the organ console. You could even build a little platform—a dozen beer-boxes will do—just inside the west door, screened as much as possible. In this sort of dramatic production, Joe has to be an artist as much as anyone else, timing his operations to accompany the actors as a pianist accompanies a singer, and he cannot do this if he is shut away in the vestry.

It may be found that the position of the electric supply may dictate the placing of the board. Very few churches have power-points and it is often necessary to go right back to the fuse-board. Give Joe time to investigate such matters and remind him that he will almost certainly need long lengths of cable to reach some of his lighting units. Sometimes it is possible to stretch cables from side to side of the building at high level, but more often than not they must be trailed across the floor, so warn him to pin them firmly down lest the vicar trip over them.

How much light shall we need? As a rough guide we can say that the minimum power needed for the audience to see the actors in an average-sized church is about 1,000 watts, though you may be able to get away with as little as 500 watts in a dark night scene, and Easter Morning will not begin to look bright and glorious at much under 3,000 watts. I generally aim to have about 2,000 watts on at each point in the play, but since all lanterns are in effect F.O.H., you will need as many lanterns as you want changes in colour and direction. This sometimes means that there are more lanterns hung than the switchboard will safely carry. In Joe's capable hands you need not worry about this, but keep any interfering busybody from putting everything on at once. The ideal to aim at is a large number of small lanterns; six at 500 watts are much more use than three at 1,000 watts, and twelve 250 watts better still. In practice, the producer has to compromise and make one unit serve in two or three different scenes, with very little left over for trick effects.

Processions

Trick effects do not come within the scope of this chapter, but processions are a prominent feature of plays in churches so I think something ought to be said about them. Remember that a procession in church has a strongly liturgical character;

a moving spot tracing it down the aisle is completely out of place and "theatrical," though it would not be so objectionable if the same play were done in a hall. The ideal method is to use two lanterns, fitted with spotting attachments and masks (the mirror-spots described on page 18), one mounted above the west door and the other as high as possible above the chancel arch. These will throw a narrow path of light along the whole length of the aisle. The hire of such units may be too expensive for you but you can do part of the job by leaving the "stage" lights on, and, if the spill of light from the acting area is not enough, bringing up some of the ordinary nave lighting. Your audience will accept that for the short time of the procession.

BETWEEN SCENES

One last plea to all beginners. Do *not* use a blackout to hide the Stage Manager rushing on to change props. Black is absence of light, not a curtain. You can either let the actors make a dignified exit carrying their furniture or properties, or direct the audience's attention away from the playing area by illuminating some architectural feature, or let the whole job be done by stage-hands while a passage of music is being played; but please do not leave the audience in the dark.

The suggestions made in this chapter may seem much too elaborate for the simple dignified production you had in mind, but remember that this is a religious play, and that nothing but the best that you and your technical assistants are capable of is good enough for God.

Concluding Note

I<small>F</small> you have read straight through this book, you will probably be in a state of confusion and despondency, confused by the intricacy of lighting and despondent at the improbability of your ever doing good work with the modest set which is all your society can afford.

But take comfort. Technical books on two of my other hobbies always have that effect on me, but I go back and look for what the author says are fundamental essentials or basic principles and consider how far I can apply them to my rudimentary equipment. I always surprise myself by finding that I can make some improvement on it, that some simple gadget I can buy or devise will extend my scope and give me better results.

I hope it will be the same with you. After all, how did you learn to produce or to design costumes or settings? By having a go, and learning from your failures. You now take these things in your stride, and so you will with lighting, even if in some ways it is the most frightening of them all to tackle. So go down to your stage, and have a good look at everything.

Imagine your play moving smoothly, in a good décor; visualize lighting that will give a satisfying picture and express your feeling about the play; go home and work on the script, adapting my suggestions to your circumstances; and on the first night you will be able to look at your show and add a private programme credit—

L<small>IGHTING</small> BY J<small>OE</small>—AND THE P<small>RODUCER</small>

Stage Lighting Firms

W. J. Furse and Co. Ltd., Traffic Street, Nottingham.
Major Equipment Co. Ltd., 22 Gorst Road, London, N.W.10.
Strand Electric and Engineering Co. Ltd., 29 King Street,
Covent Garden, London, W.C.2.

These firms will also advise on special effects which are
difficult to produce with ordinary equipment, and will hire
apparatus. This includes such things as chandeliers, torches
and oil lamps, which are sometimes awkward to devise to
conform with fire regulations.

Short Bibliography

MOST of these books can be borrowed by members from the
Library of the British Drama League, 9 Fitzroy Square,
London.

BENTHAM, FREDERICK, *Stage Lighting*. Pitman.
CORRY, P., *Lighting the Stage*. Pitman.
FARADAY, E. E., *Basic Stage Lighting and Equipment*. Furse,
Nottingham.
GOFFIN, PETER, *Stage Lighting for Amateurs*. Muller.
OST, GEOFFREY, *Stage Lighting*. Herbert Jenkins.
SAY, M. G., *Lighting the Amateur Stage*. Albyn Press, Edinburgh.
STRAND ELECTRIC AND ENGINEERING CO. LTD. (*see* above)
publish many books and pamphlets on lighting. Write to
them.
WILLIAMS, R. GILLESPIE, *The Technique of Stage Lighting*.
Pitman.
WILSON, ANGUS, *Home-made Lighting Apparatus for the Amateur
Stage*. Deane.